The Bush Theatre presents the world premiere of

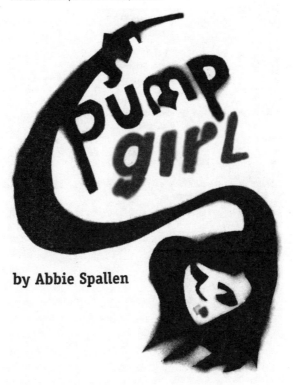

by Abbie Spallen

thebushtheatre

Cast

(in alphabetical order)

Hammy	**James Doran**
Pumpgirl	**Orla Fitzgerald**
Sinead	**Maggie Hayes**

Director	**Mike Bradwell**
Designer	**Bob Bailey**
Sound Designer	**Tanya Burns**
Assistant Director	**Meriel Baistow-Clare**
Producer	**Fiona Clark**

Press Representation	**Alexandra Gammie** **020 7837 8333**
Graphic Design	**Stem Design** **www.stemdesign.co.uk**

The Bush Theatre's world premiere production of *Pumpgirl* opened at the Traverse Theatre, at the 2006 Edinburgh Fringe Festival.

Pumpgirl received its London premiere at The Bush Theatre on 12 September 2006.

James Doran Hammy

Theatre includes *1974 (The End of Year Show), The Weir, Observe the Sons of Ulster Marching Across the Somme, Of Mice and Men, New Morning, The Hidden Curriculum, Dockers* (Lyric Theatre, Belfast), *The Secret Diary of Adrian Mole, Justice* (tours) *Black Taxis, Ragged Trousered Philanthropist, Des, The Laughter of our Children, Bin Lids, Forced Upon Us* (Dubbeljoint), *Macbeth* (Lyric Theatre /Prime Cut), *Bell, Book and Candle* (Belfast Festival), *The House of Goodwill* (Centre Stage), *Killers Head* (Belfast Theatre Company), *Juno and the Paycock* (Manchester Contact Theatre), *The Evangelist, Stags and Hens* (Arts Theatre), *Joyriders* (Sheffield Crucible) and *Endgame* (Fringe Benefits Theatre).

Television includes *Holy Cross, Pulling Moves, Rebel Heart* and *Branwen*. Film includes *Mickeybo & Me, Holy Cross, H3, Nothing Personal, A Further Gesture*, and the short films *Everything In This Country Must* (Oscar-nominated) and *Heroes*.

Radio includes *Jangle of the Keys, The Journey, Juno and the Paycock, Good Lads at Heart* (BBC Radio 4) and *Bad Girls, Good Women* (BBC Radio Ulster).

Orla Fitzgerald Pumpgirl

Film and television includes *The Wind That Shakes The Barley* (Winner of the Cannes Film Festival Palmes d'Or for Best Film 2006), *The Last Furlong, The Baby Wars, Love is the Drug, Strangers in the Night, In the Company of Strangers, Therapy* and *Loves Elusives*.

Theatre includes *This Ebony Bird* (Blood in the Alley Theatre Company), *The System* (The Project, Raw Productions), *The Day I Swapped My Dad For Two Goldfish* (The Ark), *Playboy of the Western World* (Royal Exchange Manchester), *A Town Called F**cked* (Last Serenade Theatre Company), *Macbeth* (Second Age), *A Quiet Life* (Peacock Theatre), *The River* (Meridian Theatre Company), *Who's Breaking?* (Graffitti Theatre Company), *Laodamia* (Merlin International Theatre), *Disco Pigs* (Corcadorca Theatre Company) and *Othello* (Everyman Theatre, Cork).

Radio includes Enda Walsh's *4 Big Days in the Life of Dessie Banks*.

Maggie Hayes Sinead

Theatre includes *Midden* (Rough Magic), *Troilus and Cressida* (Oxford Stage Company), *All My Sons* (Big Telly), *Northern Star* (Tinderbox/Field Day), *Translations* (Lyric Theatre), *The Evangelist, The House of Goodwill* (Centre Stage), *Exercises de Style* (CDR de Bretagne), *Andromache* (Theatre des 3 Quartiers), *Le Misanthrope, Les Maires de la tour Eiffel* (Theatre d'un Soir) and *The Plough and the Stars* (O'Casey Theatre Company).

Film and television includes *Proud, Powers, Making Waves, The Bill, Give My Head Peace* and *The Most Fertile Man in Ireland*. Radio includes *Half Sketch Half Biscuit*.

Abbie Spallen Writer

Abbie's writing credits include *Abeyance* (a 'Druid Debut' for Druid Theatre Company, directed by Kirsten Sheridan), *Alice Kyteler* (rehearsed reading; Galloglass Theatre Company), and the short plays *Two Magpies* (ESB Dublin Fringe Festival) and *Epiphany* (part of Semper Fi's 'Another 24 Hours'). She was awarded the Dublin City Council Bursary for Literature 2005, and she made the Sunday Tribune's annual 'Most Promising Young People in Irish Theatre' list in 2002. She is currently working on a screenplay, *Seven Drunken Knights*.

Abbie has also worked as an actor for over ten years in television, film and theatre, and has been nominated for the Belfast Telegraph EMA best actress award. Recent appearances include *Pavee Lackeen*, the multi-award winning feature by Perry Ogden; *The Wiremen*, a recent musical from Abhann Productions at the Gaiety Theatre, Dublin; and *1974, The End of Year Show* at the Lyric, Belfast.

Mike Bradwell Director

Mike Bradwell has been Artistic Director of The Bush Theatre for 10 years, which he has been associated with since 1974. He appeared in Mike Leigh's *Bleak Moments* and was an actor/musician with The Ken Campbell Road Show and an underwater escapologist with Hirst's Carivari. Mike founded Hull Truck Theatre Company in 1971 and directed all their shows for 10 years, including several of his own plays. He has directed more than 35 shows at The Bush, including *Love and Understanding* by Joe Penhall (also at The Long Wharf Theatre, U.S.A), *Love You, Too* by Doug Lucie, *Dead Sheep, Little Baby Nothing* and *Shang-a-Lang* by Catherine Johnson (also 1999 national tour), *Howie The Rookie* by Mark O'Rowe (also 1999 Edinburgh Festival and internationally), *Resident Alien* by Tim Fountain (also New York Theater Workshop), *Blackbird* by Adam Rapp, *Airsick* by Emma Frost, *adrenalin...heart* by Georgia Fitch (also Tram Theatre, Tokyo), *Gong Donkeys* and *The Glee Club* by Richard Cameron (also at The Duchess Theatre, the Bolton Octagon, Galway Arts Festival and on tour), *The Girl With Red Hair* by Sharman Macdonald (Edinburgh Lyceum and Hampstead Theatre), *When You Cure Me* by Jack Thorne and *crooked* by Catherine Trieschmann. Mike has also directed for other theatres including Hampstead Theatre, the Tricycle, King's Head, West Yorkshire Playhouse, The National Theatre of Brent and The Royal Court, where he was Associate Director.

Bob Bailey Designer

Work for The Bush Theatre includes *Bottle Universe, The God Botherers, Stitching* and *Hijra*.

Theatre includes *Paradise Bound* (Liverpool Everyman), *Love Me Tonight* (Hampstead Theatre), *The Lying Kind* (Royal Court, London), *Edward Gant's Amazing Feats of Loneliness* (The Drum, Plymouth), *Angels In America* and *Charley's Aunt* (Crucible Theatre, Sheffield), *All Nighter* (The Royal Ballet), *Rent* and *Cabaret* (English Theatre, Frankfurt), *Translations* and *Moll Flanders* (Theatre Royal, Bristol Old Vic), UK tours of *Anything Goes, The New Statesman, Lieutenant of Inishmore* and *The Real Thing*.

Opera includes *Manon Lescaut, Fedora, Macbeth* and *La Sonnambula* (all for Opera Holland Park), *Falstaff* (Guildhall Opera), *Tosca* (Nationale Reisopera, Netherlands) and *About Face* (Linbury Theatre, R.O.H.).

In 1999 Bob was awarded Time Out Designer of The Year for his set design for DV8's production of *The Happiest Day Of My Life* (UK and European tour).

Tanya Burns Lighting Designer

Tanya was awarded the prestigious Arts Foundation Fellowship for Lighting Designers in 1996, and has since gained her MSc in Light and Lighting at UCL's Bartlett School of Architecture. In addition to theatre, she is now a lighting consultant on exhibition, architectural and environmental projects.

Recent work includes Samsung ITU, Geneva; Samsung Centre, Moscow; Ford, Las Vegas; Nasdaq TV Studios, Times Square New York; Coca Cola at Madison Square Gardens, New York; Samsung Pavillion and Exhibition at the Winter Olympics, Salt Lake City (International Gold Award Winner).

Tanya has worked for many years in British theatre, covering the West End, London and regional repertory theatres, lighting dance and opera as well as theatre. Her most recent work for The Bush Theatre, where she is an Associate Artist, includes *When You Cure Me* by Jack Thorne, *adrenalin...heart* by Georgia Fitch and *The God Botherers* by Richard Bean.

Meriel Baistow-Clare Assistant Director

Since graduating from Oxford University and completing a masters degree at Queen Mary College, Meriel has directed a number of new plays including *Pretend You Have Big Buildings* by Ben Musgrove at E15, *Born to Run* by Amanda Whittingdon and a reading of new plays by local writers at The Bush Theatre. She has worked as an assistant director on a number of plays, including *When You Cure Me* by Jack Thorne at The Bush Theatre. She was also director of Pursued By A Bear Youth Theatre and directs short political plays at Theatre 503 once a month.

Fiona Clark Producer

Fiona is Executive Producer of The Bush Theatre and Joint Chief Executive with Mike Bradwell. Alongside seasons of new work at The Bush, Fiona is Managing Director of the theatre's commercial arm, Bush Productions Limited. Recent Bush projects include the national tour of *Mammals* by Amelia Bullmore, *After the End* by Dennis Kelly (Traverse Theatre, The Bush Theatre, national and international tour 2005/6), *The Girl With Red Hair* by Sharman Macdonald (Edinburgh Lyceum and Hampstead Theatre), *The Glee Club* by Richard Cameron (The Bush Theatre, Duchess Theatre, 2002, Galway Arts Festival and national tour, 2004), *adrenalin...heart* by Georgia Fitch (The Bush Theatre, Tokyo International Festival 2004), *Stitching* by Anthony Neilson (Edinburgh Festival, The Bush Theatre, UK and European tour, *Airsick* by Emma Frost (The Bush Theatre and Drum Theatre Plymouth), *Howie the Rookie* by Mark O'Rowe (The Bush Theatre, Edinburgh Festival, PS122 New York, Magic Theatre San Francisco) and *Resident Alien* by Tim Fountain (The Bush Theatre, New York Theatre Workshop, NY).

Prior to The Bush Theatre, she held positions as Associate Director at Theatre Royal Bath and Producer for Theatre Royal Bath Productions, Project co-ordinator for Paines Plough, Director of Northland Festival, New Zealand, Associate Director (Education) at Salisbury Playhouse, and Education Director at Bristol Old Vic.

The Bush Theatre

The Bush Theatre opened in April 1972 in the upstairs dining room of The Bush Hotel, Shepherds Bush Green. The room had previously served as Lionel Blair's dance studio. Since then, The Bush has become one of the country's leading new writing venues with over 350 productions, premiering the finest new writing talent.

Playwrights whose works have been performed at The Bush include: Stephen Poliakoff, Robert Holman, Tina Brown, Snoo Wilson, John Byrne, Ron Hutchinson, Terry Johnson, Beth Henley, Kevin Elyot, Doug Lucie, Dusty Hughes, Sharman Macdonald, Billy Roche, Tony Kushner, Catherine Johnson, Philip Ridley, Richard Cameron, Jonathan Harvey, Richard Zajdlic, Naomi Wallace, David Eldridge, Conor McPherson, Joe Penhall, Helen Blakeman, Lucy Gannon, Mark O'Rowe and Charlotte Jones.

The theatre has also attracted major acting and directing talents including Bob Hoskins, Alan Rickman, Antony Sher, Stephen Rea, Frances Barber, Lindsay Duncan, Brian Cox, Kate Beckinsale, Patricia Hodge, Simon Callow, Alison Steadman, Jim Broadbent, Tim Roth, Jane Horrocks, Gwen Taylor, Mike Leigh, Mike Figgis, Mike Newell and Richard Wilson. Victoria Wood and Julie Walters first worked together at The Bush, and Victoria wrote her first sketch on an old typewriter she found backstage.

In over 30 years, The Bush has won over one hundred awards and recently received The Peggy Ramsay Foundation Project Award. Bush plays, including most recently *The Glee Club*, have transferred to the West End. Off-Broadway transfers include *Howie the Rookie* and *Resident Alien*. Film adaptations include *Beautiful Thing* and *Disco Pigs*. Bush productions have toured throughout Britain, Europe, North America and Asia, most recently *Stitching, adrenalin...heart* (representing the UK in the Tokyo International Arts Festival, 2004), *The Glee Club* (2004), *After The End* (UK, Europe and New York, 2006) and a national number one tour of *Mammals* (2006).

Every year The Bush receives over fifteen hundred scripts through the post, and every one is read. This is one small part of a comprehensive Writers' Development Programme, which includes commissions, bursaries, one-to-one dramaturgy, masterclasses, workshops and readings.

According to The Sunday Times:

"What happens at The Bush today is at the very heart of tomorrow's theatre"

That's why we read all the scripts and will continue to do so.

Mike Bradwell
Artistic Director

Fiona Clark
Executive Producer

At The Bush Theatre

Artistic Director	**Mike Bradwell**
Executive Producer	**Fiona Clark**
Finance Manager	**Dave Smith**
Literary Manager	**Abigail Gonda**
Marketing Manager	**Nicki Marsh**
Production Manager	**Robert Holmes**
Theatre Administrator	**Nic Wass**
Resident Stage Manager	**Ros Terry**
Chief Technician	**Sam Shortt**
Literary Assistant	**Raphael Martin**
Administrative Assistant	**Lydia Fraser-Ward**
Box Office Supervisor	**Darren Elliott**
Box Office Assistants	**Gail MacLeod** **Margaret-Ann Bain**
Front of House Duty Managers	**Kellie Batchelor** **Adrian Christopher** **Catherine Nix-Collins** **Lois Tucker**
Duty Technicians	**Helen Spall** **Tom White**
Associate Artists	**Tanya Burns** **Es Devlin** **Richard Jordan** **Paul Miller**
Pearson Writer in Residence	**Jack Thorne**

The Bush Theatre
Shepherds Bush Green
London W12 8QD

Box Office: 020 7610 4224
www.bushtheatre.co.uk

The Alternative Theatre Company Ltd. (The Bush Theatre)
is a Registered Charity number: 270080
Co. registration number 1221968
VAT no. 228 3168 73

Be There At The Beginning

The Bush Theatre is a writer's theatre – dedicated to commissioning, developing and producing exclusively new plays. Up to seven writers each year are commissioned and we offer a bespoke programme of workshops and one-to-one dramaturgy to develop their plays. Our international reputation of over thirty years is built on consistently producing the very best work to the very highest standard.

With your help this work can continue to flourish.

The Bush Theatre's Patron Scheme delivers an exciting range of opportunities for individual and corporate giving, offering a closer relationship with the theatre and a wide range of benefits from ticket offers to special events. Above all, it is an ideal way to acknowledge your support for one of the world's greatest new writing theatres.

To join, please pick up an information pack from the foyer, call 020 7602 3703 or email info@bushtheatre.co.uk

We would like to thank our current members and invite you to join them.

Rookies

Anonymous
Ross Anderson
Geraldine Caufield
Nina Drucker
John Gowers
Ms Sian Hansen
Lucy Heller
Mr G Hopkinson
Joyce Hytner, ACT IV
Radfin
Casarotto Ramsay &
 Associates Ltd
Robin Kermode
Ray Miles
Mr & Mrs Malcolm Ogden
John & Jacqui Pearson
Radfin
Clare Rich
Mark Roberts
Tracey Scoffield
Martin Shenfield
Alison Winter

Beautiful Things

Anonymous
Alan Brodie
Kate Brooke
David Brooks
Clive Butler
Matthew Byam Shaw
Jeremy Conway
Clyde Cooper
Mike Figgis
Vivien Goodwin
Sheila Hancock
David Hare
Laurie Marsh
Michael McCoy
Mr & Mrs A Radcliffe
John Reynolds
Barry Serjent
John & Tita Shakeshaft
Brian D Smith
Barrie & Roxanne Wilson

Glee Club

Anonymous
Jim Broadbent
Curtis Brown Group Ltd
Alan Rickman

Handful of Stars

Gianni Alen-Buckley

Lone Star

Princess of Darkness

Bronze Corporate Membership

Anonymous
Act Productions Ltd

Silver Corporate Membership

The Agency (London) Ltd

Platinum Corporate Membership

Anonymous

Ripe and Juicy
Autumn Season 2006

Pumpgirl
by Abbie Spallen
12 Sept – 14 Oct

Three people. One wild border town.
A night of sex and violence.
Mike Bradwell directs this hot new
play fresh from the Edinburgh Festival.

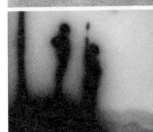

Bones
by Kay Adshead
17 Oct – 4 Nov

The acclaimed writer of *The Bogus
Woman* returns to The Bush with her
political and provocative new play
about South Africa.

Whipping It Up
by Steve Thompson
8 Nov – 16 Dec

A backstage pass into the frenetic
world of the Whips' Office in
Parliament, *Whipping It Up* is a
scandalously funny new play from the
writer of the smash-hit *Damages*.

bushpush nights

The Bush Theatre holds special student nights for school and college groups on the first Tuesday and Wednesday after each new play opens.

See great theatre for less – every 11th ticket is free when booking in a group, and student tickets for bushpush nights are just £7 (normally £10). This offer is also open to students booking individually. Student ID required.

bushpush dates for this autumn are:

Pumpgirl | 19 & 20 September | 8pm
Bones | 24 & 25 October | 8pm
Whipping It Up | 14 & 15 November | 8pm

bushpush email list

Go on, Push The Bush! Join our student email list for show updates, special offers and competitions.
Just email bushpush@bushtheatre.co.uk

For more information visit www.bushtheatre.co.uk

bushfutures
building the theatre of tomorrow...

This autumn The Bush Theatre will launch pilot schemes for its ambitious new training and development programme, bushfutures, providing opportunities for different sectors of the community to access the expertise of Bush writers, directors, designers, technicians and actors, and play an active role in the future development of the theatre.

What to look out for:

The Bush Theatre & National Student Drama Festival
Workshops and masterclasses for student companies at the Edinburgh Festival.

Company Mentoring
Advice and support for an emerging new writing company at the Edinburgh Festival, culminating in a showcase at The Bush Theatre this September.

Bush Activists
A theatre group for 16-18 year-olds, who will study acting, stage management and writing with professional practitioners.

Future Playwrights
Writing courses with Bush writers and staff, culminating in scratch showcase performances.

Futures Directors
An opportunity for new directors to work with professional directors, and participate in **bushfutures** courses.

If you'd like to find out more about how to get involved, please email bushfutures@bushtheatre.co.uk

Abbie Spallen
Pumpgirl

ff

faber and faber

First published in 2006
by Faber and Faber Limited
3 Queen Square, London WC1N 3AU

Typeset by Country Setting, Kingsdown, Kent CT14 8ES
Printed in England by Bookmarque, Croydon, Surrey

A CIP record for this book
is available from the British Library

ISBN 978-0-571-23422-6
ISBN 0-571-23422-4

2 4 6 8 10 9 7 5 3 1

In memory of my father
Ray Spallen

Characters

Pumpgirl
Sinead
Hammy

Setting

The play is set in a petrol station in present-day Ireland.

The petrol station, with a small shop attached, a fruitless attempt at a franchise, is situated a fraction over the border – in the North but only just, a location on the wrong side of a fluctuating exchange rate.

The business is on its last legs: battered, faded signs, ends curling in the sun, grace the stage: desperate attempts at enticing customers with cheap two-litre bottles of cola and free car-wax.

Pumpgirl is one of the people who work in the petrol station. She's in her twenties. A butch girl. A girl who loves her job and thinks she's one of the lads. A tomboy all growed up.

PUMPGIRL

Act One

Pumpgirl There it is. I swear. Comin' back at me across the counter. On his face as he's handin' over the money. The look. The snake-eye hyena hairy-eyeball look. He presses one sweaty, rolled up ten-pound note into my hand and he's bein' all intimate like. All chummy. As if his fingers, all clumped together in a downward pointy, like a finger fuck, as if his downward pointy fingers just touchin' the palm of my hand are hiding some sort of a sexy bond known only to the two of us. The big bollocks.

'Was that two-star or three-star, Mr McCabe?'

'Ach sure, Sandra, why don't I let you guess?'

And there it is again, there, see it? There's that wee tiny sneer makin' its way over every crease of dirty-blue skin. His top lip curls like Elvis because he's the fuckin' man. I'm checkin' the pump register and now I have to stand on tiptoe to have a gleek outside. He's watchin' me move. There's sniggers from the two, fatty and skinny, standing behind him in the queue.

'I can see your flatbed from here. Oh I forgot, of course; it'll be diesel, won't it?'

'Now don't you see what I do to her, ladies? I'm after makin' her forget herself. There's the effect I'm after havin' on the women.'

Bip-bip goes the till. I'm trying real hard not to meet his wink as he lifts his full-fat and his *Sunday World* and leaves the shop. As he passes the fatty and skinny he moves that wee bit too close to them and a gap appears, a wee, small, baby triangle of pinky blue, where the bottom of his shirt, the bit with no buttons left, squeezes his fatty flesh out over the top of his belt. He stands there like a plum with his arms in the air and his mouth puckered into the shape of an 'O'. There's a Red Indian on his brass belt-buckle, with feathers and everything. I can see this trace of hair from the top of the buckle to his belly button, black, snaking, like smoke signals.

Surprised to see him in here anyway. Diesel fucker. Surprised we get anyone in here these days. Diesel's cheaper in the South so the cars just fly on past. Or some of the garages round here wash the red. Agricultural diesel, red, stick it in the wash and who's to know, but McGiven who owns this place is too much of a chicken for that, so all I really get to do now is check oil or tyre-pressure, and most people can do that themselves. Even the women can. They started some sort of basic motor mechanics classes at the local tech. Teacher was a ride. Part-time stripper for hen nights from Keady. Class was packed. I can't stand the women drivers. They can't drive for shite. No, no, it's a fact. And they think they're hilarious. They do. There was this one time I followed this one out to her car. I was giving the oil a check. There were four of them in the car, all laughing. There were copies of *OK!* magazine in the back seat. That one, Ginger Spice or whoever she is now. The fat-thin-fat-thin one who called her baby after a slut. There was she, on the cover, lookin' fat.

Anyway, one of them in the car beckons me over. Beckons, like the Queen.

So I'm leanin' over the glass. Says she, ''Scuse me?'

'Jesus, Deirdre, don't. Don't be so mean,' comes this voice from the back.

'What can I do for you, ladies?'

Now I'm standing there smiling. I'm pushing my baseball hat round so that it sits backwards on my head because I'm a professional. Happy as you like. There was my favourite stink of petrol, sweet and sour. Not like a Chinese takeaway, more like if you got a bag of cherries and mashed them all up and then were to take the whole load and slam it into a bucket of vinegar.

'Well, we were just wondering, I mean I hope you don't mind, think we're being a bit rude, like.' I could see streaks in her fake tan round her chin where she hadn't wiped.

'Ask away.'

'Well, we were just wondering like, if you were, like, a *man* or a *woman*?'

Now they're lovin' this in the back of the car. There's shrieks and howls of laughter. Oul' 'wipe-yer-neck' Deirdre's a big hit all right.

'Well she does look a bit AC/DC, doesn't she?' Screams now from the back.

I wanted to say something smart back, but I couldn't think of anythin'. I just pushed myself off the rolled-down window and as they drove away I watched them. The two in the back were playin' air guitars.

Hammy's in the car. The car's in a race.

Hammy Ow! Ow! Ow! My fuckin' head! Ow! Jesus! My head. That hurts. Oh fuck me, that hurts. They don't call me No-Helmet for nothin'. Ow! Ah no. No-Helmet Hammy. That's me. Ow! Ow! Will I stick her into fourth? Why the fuck not? There's that sound I love. That wee crunch and groan of the gears beneath me. There's the crowd roarin' round me. The disco lights zippin' past me. Lights bouncin' off the windscreen, my head bouncin' off the side window. No-Helmet Hammy McAlinden cuttin' up the track. The pain, the ecstasy and me.

My back wheels is skiddin' on the track. That bastard McPolin's ahead of me on points but no mind to that. This is the last race of the night. This's the one they remember. The bollix on the megaphone's screaming my name over and over and No-Helmet Hammy McAlinden is gonna wipe McPolin off the face of this very planet.

'We will, we will rock you!' Do you hear that?

Is that Francie Quinn at my arse? Trying his luck.
You've no chance the night, Francie. Ah, now there's
another oul' sound I love. The sound of them oul'
windscreen-wipers screek-screekin' back and forward
against the mud on that oul' winda. No-Helmet Hammy
at the racin'. The Stock. The lads'll all be watching. Doot
the nutter and McManus, the wife's brother-in-law, and
Shawshank. Shawshank got let out of Maghaberry Prison
early by letting on he'd been born again, redeemed. Your
man in the film had to crawl through miles of shite to get
free. The Shawshank just had to spoof a load of it. There
they all are, the three amigos, all watching, jumping up
and down by now.

Francie's still at my arse. I'll move her up another gear.
More mud, crunchin' gears, screeking wipers, head
juddin' off the side window. I'm gonna have a big welt
there just above my ear, but no matter. There's that
pothole again. Nearly, hold her, hold her, squeeze her.
Now we're okay again. Francie's in the pothole now.
Serves you right for being up me arse. Well, will you look
at that, oul' Francis is twistin' round in the air. There, he's
away now, can't see him any more. He'll be skiddying
sideways, headin' for the crowd and they shittin'
themselves and then headin' away from the crowd and
them actin' like hardmen and then round and round
clippin' everything in a big ball of smoke and twisted
metal like a Spiderman cartoon or Captain Marvel or the
Fantastic Five.

Ooh ooh ooh, another one bites the dust.

Means fuck-all to me of course because I'm too busy
winnin'.

Sinead I can hear him coming in. First, like always, two
spots of light appear in each corner of the wall in front of
the bed, like aliens landing. Then when they meet in the
middle they fill the whole room with so much light that

I have to squint and even if I had been asleep I would have woken right up. A second later I hear the noise of the car, the drive up the gravel path and that way he puts the handbrake on. Hear it shudder to a stop and give that funny wee choke at the end, like an oul' man's cough. The key turns in the door and he's in. A big long sigh then, of relief. Not from me though. A big sigh of relief from him. He's made it. Safe. After he's pinballed his way up the stairs and into the room I hear him slip off his shirt and socks and leave them on a heap on the floor. I listen to him swear softly as the coins from his pocket make a clatter so I move slightly in the bed, stretch like Bagpuss, just to let him know I'm still asleep. Then he'll pause. He's probably standing there rooted to the spot, suspended, like something out of *The Matrix*, on tiptoe with one hand clutching his jeans at half-mast round his knees. The mental picture nearly makes me laugh out loud. He'll make like GI Joe across the floor and lift the covers stepping first one clammy foot and then the other into the bed beside me. One day I'm going to staple the bed clothes to the side of the bed just to let him know that every night, every night since the day and hour we were married, every night that he's gone out and come in like the Charge of the Light Brigade, I've been awake and lying like a statue with my hand stuffed in my mouth. I used to put it there to stop my crying, in the days when I gave a shite, but now it's only to stop up the laughin'.

Pumpgirl Hammy told me not to mind the ones in the car. Hammy's pure class. Hammy lives on the same estate as me. Hammy loves country music just like I do, but not Garth Brooks. The best country music is Irish country music. The best Irish country music is South Armagh country music. Pure. Hammy likes Glen Campbell though. Oul' Glen has a class voice. Hammy says that Glen's career was very hampered on account of him being labelled the housewives' choice. Hammy says that if we look at the range of his music when he was with Capitol, we can see a man of enormous varied musical talent. Far beyond the constraints of the title he was lumbered with.

(*Sings.*) 'By the time I get to Phoenix she'll be risin' . . .'

Hammy's wife is a pure cunt. No, she is. I swear. I wouldn't lie. She doesn't deserve him. He's two kids. A wee boy and a wee girl. Hammy only stays because of the kids. Says he'd leave her in a flash if he didn't have the kids, and that's fair enough. Hammy works in the local chicken hatcheries but the dole don't know. Hammy comes into the garage nearly every day. You can hear him a mile off: brakes screaming, horn blaring. It's a musical horn. Hammy likes to soup up old cars. Seventies jobs. He has a souped-up old Toyota Celica, navy blue with wee bits of silver fleck in the paint. When you're leaning over to fill the petrol tank you can smell the heat on the paint as the sun glints off the disco sparklies in the roof. Hammy always lets *me* fill up the car. I mean, what am I here for? Then he follows me into the shop for a wee chat.

'How's the cunt?' says I, meaning his wife. It's always the same.

'Still a cunt,' says he and we laugh.

'How's the cunt?' says he, meaning my cunt.

'Still a cunt,' says I. It's our wee game.

There isn't a person in the whole world I can talk to like Hammy. I'm that glad he's my friend. He always stays far longer in the shop than he has to, just chatting. Hammy does a bit of racing at the stock-car track up by the new hotel that got bombed in '94. I've never been myself, but Hammy tells me all about it. He leans over the counter chatting away, letting his fingers run through the loose 5p sweets on the counter. McGiven, who owns the shop, is a mad one for getting the out-of-date boxes of Cadbury's Roses and opening them and settin' them on the counter for mugs to buy for 5p each. And it works too. There they all are, shelling out 5p a sweet not knowing that they're out-of-date big time and that Hammy McAlinden has just rubbed two weeks of oil changes all over them. When Hammy leaves, I always place the sweets in the prime position on the counter for a big sell.

Hammy Ah, McPolin's giving me daggers all right as I'm makin' my way onto the winners' podium. Podium my arse. A few mouldy oul' teetering Jaffa orange-boxes stacked up against a wall with a bit of green fake lawn flung over them. I am the almighty hero of the year standing up here, a bit wobbly like but nothing I can't handle, just standing up here waiting for my name to be called out.

'And tonight's second prize on points, but also the winner of the last race of the night goes to, for the second time this month, local boy Hammy "No-Helmet" McAlpine.' McAlpine? They're blabbing the wrong name through the mike! The lads are pissin' themselves at this. McPolin looks delighted with himself. Doot and McManus are waving lighters and Shawshank has an oul' scarf. He's standing there waving it slowly like he's at a Bruce Springsteen concert. The bit of green-plastic lawn at my feet begins to shake and move. The voice on the megaphone is blabbin' away 'Sponsored by Grant's Nurseries, for all your gardening needs. Turn left at the bypass, bargains in all fuckin' potted plants, miniature playground available for the kids.' And there's me. Hammy No-Helmet whatever-my-name-is standin' up here with a fake grin on my face wantin' to bounce that retard with the mike off the walls.

Sinead He smells of beer, and cigarettes and milk. He's drank the last of the milk then. Hope it turns to cheese in his stomach. I'll have to go to the shops tomorrow. Or tomorrow's Wednesday. The mobile shop comes round

at eleven. The kids can have toast and he can do without.
Ah, lateral thinking, the curse of the modern mother.
'Spell *lateral*, Hammy,' I want to shout. Or even better,
'What does it mean, Hammy, go on, tell us?' Then, in my
mind, I run to the cooker and press the timer button so
that it makes that game-show noise. Dnnnnnnnnnng!!!!
'Time's up, Hammy, you thick bastard, but then you
always were a thick bastard, weren't you?'

He smells of something else too. Aftershave and diesel
and sweaty woman.

I can feel the first of his low snores beginning to form
from the pillow beside me. His bottom lip goes in and
out with each snore, like a baby's. I used to think that
was cute.

'Your honour. It was the way his bottom lip puckered
when he snored that made me put the hatchet through his
head.'

How's that for a country and western song, Hammy?
I could call it 'And I'm Praying for a Female Judge'.

The snores are getting louder. There's a large red welt
on the side of his head. His breath feels rancid on my
cheek. I'll have to change that pillowcase in the morning.
Does he never notice the new pillowcase practically every
night on his side of the bed? A different colour, totally
different pattern to the rest of the bedclothes? If I could
saw the bed in half I would. There's those rich couples,
aren't there, who have different rooms to sleep in? I read
once where Michael Caine and the wife, the one he'd
picked off the TV from that coffee ad, they have different
halves of the same house to live in. What's her name?
Oh aye, Shakira. One minute she's dancing about, waving
a few coffee beans round her head and the next minute
she's half a house for just herself, and the husband on the
other side needing permission to come in. 'No, you're all
right there, Michael, I don't feel like visitors today. Now
fuck off.'

Hammy steps off the podium.

Hammy I've had enough of this. I'll jus' leave McPolin up there looking like a sad bastard. I should really have waited till the overall winner steps off first, but what can I say? As I'm steppin' down the bit of lawn from Grant's Nurseries shifts around again and it's McPolin's turn to steady himself against the wall. There's a wee vein bulging' away in his temple. I'm makin' my way through the crowd who don't know my name anyway and they're all slappin' me on the back so I feel a wee bit better. Two young ones, one with braces like a set of train-tracks, come up to me for my autograph. Autographs. They have a book and a pencil and everything. I exchange a few pleasantries – 'Can you get Sky Sports on them, love?' – and make my way to the bar. I'm sippin' away on a pint of Bud and the lads are on their way over but then they stop. They're pissin' themselves laughin' again and holdin' each other up. What the fuck's goin' on, I'm thinkin', and then something catches my eye. Ah, would you look at that fuck. Her da's in. Oul' man-woman's da. Oul' Pumpgirl from the garage's da is at the bar. This is not my fuckin' night. He's lookin' like he wants to have a conversation but is havin' a bit of bother standin' up. He's using the bar to steady himself and his right knee's bucking away with the tremors. Shawshank's lookin' like he's goin' to have a heart attack with the hilarity of it all so I ignore the swayin' lump of alcho-shite and turn to this blonde one standing beside me.

'What do you think of my trophy?'

'Go fuck yourself.'

The ice bitch. The stuck-up cow. I'll bet she's not a real blonde. Look at her. Marilyn from the back, Manson from the front. I have a massive hard-on.

Sinead is in another part of the stage. A kitchen area. She picks up the little trophy in front of her on a table.

19

She gets a skewer from the kitchen drawer and happily scrawls, taking her time, onto the plaque at the bottom of the trophy.

Sinead (*scrawl*) 'W' . . . (*scrawl*) 'A' . . . (*scrawl*) 'N' . . .

Pumpgirl Sometimes Hammy turns up at the garage just before the end of my shift. Like magic. Then he gives me a lift home. 'Seems only right,' says he, on account of us living in the same place. Sometimes Hammy makes a detour up the loanie to our spot, left of the hatcheries and beside that oul' burnt out library van. That's our spot. It was where two Prods were took and killed about fifteen years ago. Their families have stuck wreaths and things onto the trees. It looks well. Hammy would smoke rollies and would offer me some. I say yes, but they make me shake like a mad thing so I only smoke half and nip the butt. Then we fuck. Hammy pulls the front seat down and lies on top of me. I don't move much. While I'm lying there, watching my feet flappin' away just either side of his ears, there's these marks I can see in the plastic on the ceiling of the car. Hammy's kids, probably. Hammy's muttering away into my ear and these marks I can see behind my flappy feet put me in mind me of this story I was told of this car that had gone into the bog up round Camlough. The people had been trapped inside. The car sank with them in it and they were there for ages, stuck, air running out, but no one could see it from the road except maybe the number plate and only if you were lookin'. And when the car was dragged out they found marks in the ceiling, like animal scratches, and bits of the beigy white roof-plastic under the fingernails of the people inside. They'd tried to claw their way out of the car while they were dying in the dark. The back of Hammy's car smells of Tayto cheese and onion. While I'm lying there lookin' to the side, because he's squashing my face, I can see bits of crisp down the sides of the seats, bits of salt in the stitchin'. But you couldn't eat them crisps; they'd taste soft and shite. Hammy pulls out before he cums. He always pulls out. He's like that. Better to be safe than sorry, he'd say.

Hammy I pull out before I came. I always pull out. Better safe than sorry. I cough, roll away from her and shimmy up my jeans. She's fishin' around in her handbag for a tissue. I was right, though, she's no blonde.

He smiles to himself.

She's chucked the tissue out the window and lit herself a cigarette.
    'Do you mind not smoking in here?'
    She's givin' me some look.
    'You smoke. You've been smoking all night.'
    'Aye, but not here, you'll stink out my motor.' Stand outside if you want to smoke.'
    She's chucked the fag out the window. Probably worried I'll drive off and leave her here. She's right.

He picks up the trophy from the floor.

Would you look at that? Probably one of them cheap ones from Quinns' sport shop beside the bus depot. There was this thick fuck in our school, ginger, one you'd batter for fun. He'd gone and bought himself a load of those trophies and let on that he'd won them. Inscribed his own name on them. One a week from whatever bit of money he made from some crap job collecting pallets. Stuck them all round the house. Thought he'd be the big man, that the women would be hanging out of him on account of he was such a big sportsman. Daley Thompson. Only ginger. Sat there every week scraping his name on with the broken blade of an oul' Swiss army-knife. Then he'd put them up on the MFI dresser, all polished and sparkling. He had trophies for everything. He was the all-round athlete. Ireland's great white and ginger hope.

Wouldn't have been so bad if he'd stuck to Gaelic or hurling, but he had ones for skiing up there. They had no inside toilet but he had a trophy for skiing. Ginger cunt.

Speaking of which maybe this is his sister.

'Do you do much sport, love?'

'What?'

'Do you do much sport? Are you the sporty type? It's a simple question, you don't have to sit there like I'm demented, are you into your sports or what?'

'Are you one of those kinky fuckers? I'm not pissing on you.'

She's a riot this one, isn't she?

'What time's your bus at?'

'Bus?'

I open the passenger door to let the lady out of the carriage. She gets out of the car with her knees together, as if there's fifteen paparazzi standing outside.

'You're a real bastard, you know that?'

'Yeah, but I'm crying inside.'

I have an urge to fuck the trophy at her but I keep it beside me. Give it to the kids. Make them proud.

Sinead is still scrawling away on the trophy.

Sinead (*scrawl*) . . . 'K' . . . (*scrawl*) 'E' . . . (*scrawl*) 'R'. Now.

She breaks the car off the trophy.

Pumpgirl Hammy called to make sure I was here. A phone-call like, on the phone on the wall. A phone-call for me. Said he'd pick me up in an hour or so, around nine. It's like a real date or something. It's on account of it being his birthday. Usually just turns up. I had to ask Louise in the garage if she'd cover for me after he rang, but she said yes. Fuck-all goin' on round here anyway. Just filling up born-agains on the way to some holy-rollers' wave-about-in-your-seat religious do. Happy-clappy in some barn or other. Too holy to know about sterling-for-euro differences and cheaper diesel two hundred yards up the road.

Said he'd pick me up around nine, but he was late, and when he did he had his mates in the car. Maybe they were on for a lift somewhere.

He grins like fuck at me when he leaps out of the car.

'How's the cunt?' says he.

'Go fuck yourself, late boy,' says I, but I'm smiling, which is a good job because Hammy's grin slips for a wee second.

The inside of the car smells of Friar Tuck's chicken burgers and coleslaw, and the dash is full of salt bags. Someone's had one of them silver boxes away, the ones with the wee white paper-towels in, that sits on the counter. I wouldn't mind that for the house. I'm just thinkin' I'll ask later when McManus, the one with the body too long for his legs, starts usin' it as an ashtray. Thinks he's Mel Gibson, this one. Has his fags tucked into the sleeve of his T-shirt. There's salad cream on his moustache and a bit of carrot stuck in one of the curls of his *Lethal Weapon* hairdo.

Shawshank McCabe was there too, givin' it billy with the look. That same oul' glad-eye stare from when he comes into the garage. The oul' coyote face that's not for good-lookin' girls. They get a different look. More like shy. This oul' gander goes with a full-fat-milk belly and a copy of the *Sunday World* and is just for the likes of me. Gleekin' away. Jukin' on his oul' neck. He's gonna twist it off in a minute. Eyes goin' right through my head and flappin' somewhere round the back of my earlobes. He's neckin' a bottle of Harp and for some reason thinks I'm deaf.

'You're lookin' very well these days, Pumpy, aren't you, sweetheart?'

'What did he fuckin' call me?'

'Ach, what's wrong, sweetheart? Do you not like being called sweetheart? Here, Hamburger, she doesn't like being ma sweetheart, what do you say to that, eh?'

Hammy passes me a bottle of beer, but he's not lookin'. An oul' fellah on the side of the road's just given us the nod that the police are round the corner so he's doin' a U-ey and beatin' up a wee dirt road. Shawshank's spilled his beer on his jeans. Hammy says, 'Fucksakes, Shank, they're only lookin' at tax discs. There's no need to piss yourself there.'

McManus laughs, Doot laughs, Hammy laughs and after a bit, Shawshank laughs too, but when I start to laugh they all stop.

Sinead Our youngest Diane gave me this book on *Women Who Love Too Much*. Although in her case it should be called 'Women who love too often'. Or 'Women who'll love for a spin round Camlough Lake and a tray of curry chips'. This book says it's it in your genes like cancer or baldy men. The kind of men you end up with. Patterns. Makes you think though, doesn't it? I mean, some women are going to get picked off the telly, aren't they, and given half a house. I get a hotpress full of pillowcases and a plastic trophy. I've a family full of women settled for a bunch of bastards. Patterns. Christmas Day at our house, *Hammer House of Horrors* wax museum open day. Mammy mammy, the TV reception's on the blink. Oh, that'll be the bolt in your uncle's neck, love.

Hammy I have to adjust my mirror to keep an eye on the cunt in the back. There's mutterin' goin' on and it's just out of my earshot and I'm strainin' to hear but there's this stupid voice comin' from my left and it's hers. And there in the back is the Shank. The chief mutterer in the back seat of the car with McManus deputy mutterer at his side and Doot the third in command, and they're all lovin' this. Shank's grinnin' away. Top lip curled, tongue pressed up against his front teeth, two missing, the tongue spreads through, white, red, white, red. He laughs, and as he does spit comes out of the side of his mouth. There she is beside me, giving it the big Lady Diana queen-of-fuckin'-hearts eyes and I'm trying to get rid of the sinkin' feelin' that I've just been had. That I've just been played like buckaroo. Sittin' in McLogan's and all innocent it starts. Shawshank's all pally-wally, sayin' to me stuff about women, women he's had. Conversation goes on and on and becomes a bit more of a competition. He's comin' out with some Fantasy Island bullshit guff about some PE teacher he's riding in Lisleagh. McManus starts chippin' in about this mother and daughter combo he's takin' turns with in Culloville. Shawshank comes right back at him with some housewife he's just left not two hours ago with a smile on her face like Liberace in a locker room. Doot's throwin' in his 50p, too, some English bird, manager of Dixons, gets him free blank videos, but they don't stay blank for long. And we're all laughin' and drinkin' and telling our oul' confessions and they're suddenly all lookin' at me. Waitin' for my contribution. For me to throw my odds into the pot. Of course, hindsight's a fuckin' wonderful thing, isn't it? Looking back now I can see what they're up to and there's a mean sore bubble of sick right in the crease of my belly. I can still hear the fucker's voice sayin', 'What about your woman up in the garage? The pumpgirl? The one who walks like John Wayne and looks like his horse?'

And he's laughin' away and they're all slappin' me on the back and off I go with the ins and outs and I'm sitting there with a trophy on my mantelpiece for fucking skiing and the boasts are getting louder and more and more red hot and Dutch, and the only one getting fucked here is me. He's sayin', 'I bet she goes now, does she? I mean, I'm not invadin' yer privacy am I, here, I mean I heard a rumour like, I mean, maybe it's not true. If it's not, sure,

I'll mind my own business. But there's no smoke without fire and there's no fire without an insurance claim if you know what I mean.'

Pumpgirl Shawshank is the most borin' man I have ever come across in my entire short life. Talks bollox all the time with a 'Am I now?' or 'Could I be?' or 'Correct me if I'm wrong, if I may?' Fuckin' eejit plum. Waste of fat space in the back of the car, borin' his way up the Lisgullion Hills. Man probably bored his way out of jail. (*She puts on an RUC voice.*) 'Here Samuel, give that one early release will you for fuck's sake, my ears is bleedin' here.'

Hammy's very quiet. I'm feelin' a bit radio 'cos there's a spliff goin' round. The beer's makin' me rift which makes Shawshank laugh himself stupid. Hammy tells me to stop riftin' so I stop.

The doorbell rings.

Sinead That'll be our Diane now, to take the kids. I sometimes get her to do that of a Thursday or a Saturday. Round about five o'clock, then I'm off.

She moves to another part of the stage.

There's this lovely time, you know, it's about five o'clock in the evening when if I have a chance at all, if I can get away from the kids, I'll ask our Diane to give them a mind and then off I go down to the market of all places. Not to buy anything, there's nothin' left. I just wander round listening to all the banter going on between the ones as they're packin' up for the day. It's a tired banter but glad to be goin' home, I suppose. Packin' up boxes full of tat and clothes, the fruit men long gone, sharp as tacks them fellahs, from Belfast mostly, no hangin' round for the last sell with them ones. And it's a nice time, the place deserted; wooden stalls bouncin' laughs and a smell of gone-off oranges and secondhand clothes. No one even notices you movin' between the stalls, they're too busy pickin' up the odd bit of china that hasn't been wrapped up to go yet. It's like as if you're a ghost or something and they pay you no mind. Maybe they think you're up for a bargain but if they do they never say. I'm wandering round this day, leanin' up against a stall sellin' yards of fake leather and caterpillar boots when there's this presence beside me.

'I do see you comin' in here a lot,' says the presence.

Fuck me, says I (to myself).

'Yeah, I like the solitude,' is what I says to the presence.

I'm lookin at him like 'sol-it-ude' might be far too big a word for the likes of this wee roundy git, I mean, I've seen him around, you know? Laughing with the lads, flickin' the ash and rockin' back and forward on his heels takin' the mick out of some tidy wee girl they'll never have. In this town you're either a slut or a snob, no in-betweens. And this is what I'm thinkin', very unkind, I know, and serves me right because then he fixes me with a grin and says, 'Whosoever is delighted in solitude is either a wild beast or a god.'

Now at this point I've nearly fell into the stall behind me. The shock makes me lean so far back that I sent a pair of Adidas green-stripe arse over tit into a puddle and he moves closer to make sure I'm okay, and there he is just lookin' at me, so I says, because I can't think of anything else to say, 'That's fierce nice, who was it said that now?' And he says, 'Francis Bacon,' and I noddin' away like I have a clue who he's talkin' about. Serves me right for my big solitude three-syllable superiority buzz, and I stand there trying not to giggle like a wee girl at school. Now there's a gap of about three seconds when he's just lookin' at me with a smile on his face and then here's he.

'Which would you be now, a goddess or a wild beast?

The wee midgety woman with a beardy chin who owns the stall appears at his shoulder and glares at me, so there's the two of them waitin' for an answer, but then I realise she's only givin' me shrapnel stares over her oul' soggy green-stripe gutties, so I looks him right in the eye and, says I, all sexy like, 'Well now, seein' as your askin', I reckon I'm a bit of both when I want to be,' and there it is, this feelin' in my insides, a scary trembling feeling I haven't had in years. Who'd have thought in the middle of Newry Market outside the secondhand record shops and next to the boiled sweets I'd have felt the first signs in years that Lawrence of Arabia wasn't in fact about to gallop on a camel through the dry dusty plains of what I lovingly like to call my old Gobi Desert down below.

Hammy Bastard's house is about here somewhere. Just leave them off, say bye-byes all laughy-smiley and grab her even if she's after stoppin' for a piss or anything, get out of here. Here's the turnin', 'Lake View'. Sweet sufferin' Jesus. 'Lake View'. Not a lake in sight. Couldn't get more landlocked if we tried. Aye, lake view all right if you ran up the side of thon' mountain to where the army look-out post was and asked them politely if they wouldn't mind now that they've fuck-all to do, if they'd let you shimmy up to the top of what's left of the tower and hang you there by your bootstraps and you might get a gleek through an oul' telescope at the edge of Camlough Lake about fifteen miles away in the North. Or maybe they'd have a few left-over photographs knockin' about. Stick them on the wall. Lovely. Lake View all right, aerial-style with bloody night vision. Some house, though. Three storeys, chaletty type of a roof, nice brickwork, eagle's heads on either side of the gate, the lot. Must be loads of money in the scrap, then. Yard looks like a scrapheap, too. Fridges, tractors, oul' cars, boilers stacked, nicked for the copper, caravan he's after breedin' a dose of pups in and a boat. A fuckin' boat. That'll be for sailin' on the lake, then.

Sinead I googled Francis Bacon. Our Diane showed me how. I thought I was thick – she was spelling it 'France's Bacon' as in 'pork products from France' till I put her right. The face on her when I tell her he's a poet. 'Why in the name of God are you googlin' the likes of him?' she says as she clicks the mouse onto 'horoscopes for celebrity babies with stupid names', and there's this wee excited voice inside my head sayin', 'Why indeed?'

Hammy Sweet Jesus, he's manhandlin' me in the door. His wife's away on a weekend in Dublin to watch an INXS tribute band and he's givin' me that look as if he's sayin', 'What, are you too scared? Dying to get away? Birthday party? Previous appointment?' 'Aye,' he says, 'Maybe her ladyship wants to get away for a manicure, Brazilian or a Back, Sack and Crack.' I'm lookin' at her leanin' out the passenger door of the car. She's rat-arsed by now. Her head bobs up and down as she tries to focus on scrapin' the butts out of some paper-towel holder McManus robbed earlier and there's salad cream and fag ash on her hands.

Sinead There's a wee Romanian gypsy woman smilin' up at me beside a selection of multipack tights. She's found herself an abandoned box of tomatoes and is havin' a good rifle through. 'Good luck to ye, love,' says I to myself, because it wasn't tomatoes I came here for. I'm movin' slowly, casual, through the stalls of the market now and tryin' to look as if I'm not lookin' round me for one person in particular. I'm just about to head, a voice inside my head askin', 'What are you at, woman? Hangin' round a dead market at five in the evening on the off-chance that you might get a sad flirt with a short squat wee thing of a man?' Because believe me he is no picture. But that's what makes it so strange. It's certainly not a looks thing. God, I'm really about to head now, feeling like a real idiot when I see him loading up a flatbed full of gypsy skirts.

'Oh, do you work here, then?' says I, actin' all surprised.

'I'm just helpin' out,' he says. 'The wife's sister owns the stall. They're a bit short-staffed at the minute.'

Now I know his wife, name of Eileen. Word is she's playin' away with a Chinese deliveryman out of Silverbridge. She has a bucket mouth and a set of fake boobs she bought in Lithuania or the like. Cost her three hundred euro and ten tops off a Rice Krispies box.

There he is, finished loadin' up the boxes now, and he turns to catch up with me walkin' away. 'What's your hurry?' he says, so I stop and say, 'No hurry, really, I'm just not hangin' around to watch you work.' He follows me down the side of the stalls and as we reach the main gate at the back of the market he gives me a cigarette and then floors me by saying. 'This is my favourite time of the market, you know?' And I say, 'Yes, yes. I do.'

We get to chattin' about this and that, although not about poetry, thank God, and as I gradually relax he asks me about Hammy.

'He's a strange one, your husband.'

There's no reply to this from me, so he thinks he's offended me. He puts his hand on my arm, and as this is the first time he's touched me I shudder inside, which he notices. He says he's sorry, it's just that he can't understand how a woman like me can end up with a man like Hammy and I want to say there wasn't much to choose from, in fact there still isn't, and I know that's real bigheaded and I don't mean to be, but why am I standing there talking to him? It's like when you've had cider all your life and someone buys you Asti Spumante you'll convince yourself you're drinkin' champagne.

Pumpgirl Shawshank's house is like a palace. Looks like *Home Front* have been or *Changin' Rooms*, only done with money. He's got pine everythin' borders and a bidet. I'm not being very well in the toilet, and this image of

Shawshank washin' his arse makes me even worse. I can hear Hammy downstairs getting the guided tour. He's saying 'Friggin' magic' and 'Champion', and Doot keeps shoutin' up the stairs, 'You okay, Pumpgirl?' My head is reelin'. There's a wee Nemo on the bathtub, and I think it talks, but I'm too dizzy to pull on the cord. I'm too busy trying to get up and get on me. My combats are nearly up when I trip over some fluffy mat and bang my teeth on the side of the bath. I have to do an assault course down the stairs past McManus who stinks of vinegar. I'm outside and there's the car. I'm inside the car on the sweaty leather seats but it's okay because I'm lying down, and if I try really hard to control my breathing, one-two one-two, and use one hand to keep an eye open, I should be okay. Hammy can do his 'Ooh aahs' and his 'Isn't that class?' and then maybe get the hell out of there and take me home.

Sinead Back in the house he opens the bottle of champagne. Its six o'clock in the evening and our Diane'll have the kids till eight. No chance of Hammy home before chuckin'-out time, specially not on his birthday, and I'm sittin' on our sofa drinkin' with a man I hardly know. For the first time in long long years there's a fire racin' round my body. I feel like when I was sixteen and would go drinkin' round the back of the new leisure centre, only it's not such a new leisure centre now, and this time I'm not cold, I'm warm. I'm very warm and the bubbles go down the wrong way making me cough.

He's a bit of a talker all right, but no mind to me. No one's talked to me like that in years. It's funny – I suppose most women want a man who'll listen. I just want one who'll fill the silence that's there between me and Hammy. The one with swearwords full of hate hangin' in the air makin' a smell like mould, like washin' left too long in the machine then hung out to dry. He takes me by the hand and leads me up the stairs and I let him. There's one of our Kelly's skates on the hall stairs and he near goes on his hoop and we laugh, dead romantic, not. 'If I ended up in traction would you visit me?' he asks, and I swear blind I would.

He's backin' his way into the kids' bedroom so I have to manoeuvre, sort of in a sexy way, him towards the spare room. I'm not doing' this on the marital bed, okay? I'm just not. And anyway the spare room's tidier on account of we never have any visitors, at least this is what I'm thinkin', only I've forgotten Hammy's fitness equipment and as my lover stubs his toe on a dumbbell I'm wondering if the poor man's going to make it out alive.

His belt-buckle off his trousers falls hard on the wooden floor with a right oul' clatter as he stands there clutching' at himself. It's a ridiculous buckle, too. Stupid-lookin' thing with an Indian head on it and everything. It's a wonder it doesn't cut his spleen in half when he sits on a chair.

Hammy 'Take a look at my girlfriend. She's the only one I got.'

Can't believe the bastard's doin' this. He's got me welded to the sofa and there's a mug of whiskey in my hand. It's one of them strip-mugs where the woman's clothes are comin' off when you pour in hot water, but the whiskey's cold so she doesn't get to do her thing. Shawshank's at the hi-fi and he's puttin on this oul' Supertramp CD with this big grin on his face. Behind him on the shelf is about twenty books of quotations. This is what the bastard does – he learns off quotations from poems and shit and then uses them to get the women into bed. Started learnin' them in Maghaberry. Smart fucker. There's this clatter down the stairs and they all laugh as 'Take a look at my girlfriend' stumbles past the open door of the sitting room and out into the yard. I take a long hard suck on the whiskey and the slut on the cup

32

looks more and more disappointed at keeping on her knickers. Shawshank stands at the Mexican-pine hi-fi unit and presses replay for the fourth time in a row. And they're all singing along now.

'Not much of a girlfriend, I never seem to get a lot.'

Pumpgirl I'm lying on the back seat with my head down on the cracks filled with crisps. I'm holding the one eye open with a finger and out of the corner of the one eye open I can see something in the glove compartment beside me. It's a shiny thing, a glittery movin' thing, and I can't properly see what it is. There's no one about and the car is warm and comfy and I think I'm feeling not too bad as I lift my head up to get a better look. In goes the hand into the glove compartment. This thing, whatever it is, keeps disappearing and coming back in front of my eyes. I can't seem to get a hold, of it but it's okay because I'm laughin' away. A glittery shiny thing. My hand is batting about in the glove compartment and I take my hand out and it's wet. But it's okay that it's wet because that's just the way it is in the warm car. There's this tiny flash and I can see what it is. A tiny fish, striped, bright gold and silver just like Nemo, jumps up and down in the glove compartment, which is full of water and stretched out transparent and plastic like a pet-shop bag. It's lovely. Gold and silver tiny fish darting about bangin' into the sides of a stretchy clear bag. I try to put my hand in again but I can't. Something's stopping it. Something's holding my hand down. I want to lift out the wee gold Nemo fish but my hand, both my hands, are trapped over my head.

Sinead My hands are stuck over my head as my jumper gets caught in his watch-strap. He undresses me with so much love, so much kindness, that I want to cry, but I don't because that's usually not a good idea when you're in bed with a fellah, so I bite my lip and then I bite his which he seems to like, which makes me laugh. There is in fact a lot of giggling going on as we get caught in bedclothes, and holy Jesus, I find a cold Dinosaur Bite under the pillow one of the kids or the dog has stashed for later. He kisses my stomach even though it's like an onion bag from two pregnancies, and I think for seconds, maybe even a minute, I'm going to be able to forget about being someone's wife, a ma or just a woman doin' something that's bad, because it is bad, isn't it? I mean, I'm bad. But there's a gap. Just enough. A gap that's filled with nothing. I get my moment. I lose myself as the fear, the grief, the loneliness, the hate on the washing-line, and the sol-it-ude slips from my mind as I feel the first of the low shudders of my body in the barely slept-in sheets of our spare bed, while the kids are with our Diane and my husband is so far away from my mind that I can't even picture his face.

Pumpgirl Hammy stands watching as Shawshank's mouth is pressed against mine. His tongue is licking round me and his breath tastes of tin. The fish has gone now and the car is back to cold and damp and dark, and this weight is pressing on my chest as he makes another grab for my hands. The Indian buckle is pressing on my belly as he pulls open my combats. My face is pressed into the back of the seat now as he turns me over. The leather sticks and then unsticks to my face. I look up at the glove compartment now but it just sits there, a manual sticking out and above it more scratches, probably Hammy's kids I'm thinkin'. I'm turned round again, and this time it's McManus. Hammy's standing behind him with this mad face on and I can't help feeling I've done something wrong. I want to tell him about my mad shiny fish dream, but I can't because there's a hand over my mouth. A hand that tastes of dirt and salt and cigarettes.

Sinead There's a smell from his armpit as he snuggles me in next to him after the sex. It's a rank musky smell of onions and sweat and I want him to go, but there's false conversation to be made. I ask him how he got the nickname Shawshank and he starts to tell me about prison. That's where he read the poetry, I ask. He looks at me and laughs and says 'Aye'. There's kids playing outside Kerb-to-Kerb, and the thump-thump of the football gives a rhythm to the awkward silence between us in the bed.

Pumpgirl And I can't help thinking of the people whose car went into the bog. My head is moving back and forward and I'm looking at the scratches on the roof above. Four people on a night out in Warrenpoint. Four people scratchin' on the roof of a car. Broken fingernails, silent screams, stiletto shoes and Saturday-night boots banging against black squeezing windows. Hammy is the last, and when he stops he rests his head beside me and he looks so sad I whisper in his ear, 'It's okay.'

Sinead Finally he gets up and puts on his clothes. He says he's sorry he has to go but he has friends to meet. It's a prearranged appointment with a few buddies. He'd stay, he really would, but his life wouldn't be worth living, now I tell no lie, if I let down my comrades, you know? And as he heads off to McLogan's I sink back into the bed. When the door slams down below I swing my legs out and head down the stairs. I clear away the glasses, I light a match. The gas comes on with a whoosh; I chuck the match into the sink. It's a quarter past seven, the kids'll be home soon and I start to make them their tea.

Blackout.

Act Two

Pumpgirl I go to work every day. Oil changes, air pressure, cherry petrol, diesel fumes, sweets on the counter for a big sell. No sign of Hammy. Keep listening out for a screech of brakes but no sign. Sometimes hear something I think is him and I run to the end of the counter, don't even flip the lid but shimmy underneath. Thinkin' it'll be him. He'll come into the garage and ask the same old question and we'll fall about the place and the fatty and skinny sisters in the queue will look at each other and tut-tut and all the time them squeezin' a loaf of bread to see if it's fresh, but we'll laugh because we know it's really because they don't get enough sex.

He lay all night passed out in the car beside me and when he woke up around nine in the morning, after we found his keys, he started the car and we headed back to town.

Hammy The longest fucking journey of my life. The car as if it's attached to Shawshank's house by some sort of big elastic as we drove past the Carrickdale Hotel and up towards the border which seemed to be moving away with every inch. Like the Brits are redrawing it and going round them farms in Crossmaglen instead of chopping right through them. A movement beside me. Light a cigarette and turn on the radio. The music fills the car, but it won't fill the silence. It does the opposite. Makes the car seem very small and very packed with her and me. Her eyes slant down at the sides. They're a grey colour. I've never noticed that before. After I leaves her, sit outside the house for a while, just smoking butt-to-butt fags. There's weans runnin' about and being took to a play group. The twenty-year-old play leader is a ride but I'm not payin' her no mind. Every time someone comes near the car I fumbles around in the dash as if I've lost something. Finally I've run out of fags and I make my way into the house. The wife is lookin' at me with a half-smile on her lips. I makes my way up the stairs and collapse on the bed. I turn round and I notice that the pillowcase under my head is different from the one beside me. I never noticed that before either.

Sinead I can hear him coming in. First, like always, two spots of light appear in each corner of the wall. Then they meet in the middle and fill the whole room with light. Then I hear the drive up the gravel path and then the handbrake on, the shudder and the oul' man's cough. Except that night I didn't. That night I heard nothing. He stayed out all night. He's never stayed out all night before, birthday or no. Always managed to make it back before the passion disco car turns into a pumpkin. I tidied the house after Shawshank went, waited smokin' cigarettes for the two kids to arrive, and then fed, washed, minded, said 'Aye right' and 'Don't pull the dog's tail' and the other pieces of robot crap that tumble out of the mouths of mas while all the time I'm thinkin' about the twinges of evidence still fresh between my legs. Like a drinker back off the wagon. Smilin' a guilty caught-on-camera look of 'naughty naughty' and awareness of totally fucked-up consequences to come. Oh my God, the fucking drama. I wonder should I have a laugh with this. Maybe a confrontation, accuse him of having an affair, you know, just to make me feel alive, or maybe because I'm supposed to give a fuck. Maybe I'll have a look in one of our one's self-help books and see if it says what to do when he arrives home at ten o'clock in the morning with a face on him like a sheep and sits in the car for an hour and a half so that the whole street is wondering what the fuck he's at. I wonder if she would have a book about that or maybe another one, thick enough to belt him round the head with.

Hammy Ow ow ow. My fuckin' head. My head is screamin' with the pain as it's juddin' off the window. The pain is screamin' through my ear and I'm havin' to clench my teeth because the sweat and blood from a laceration over my eye is seepin' down into the socket. I'm tryin' to find something to wipe my eyes, but my gloves are filthy so oil goes in them, which is just fuckin' lovely. McPolin is at my arse. I can feel him prangin' away at the bumper. Hold on till I wipe my eyes, you prangin' prick, but he won't of course, and comin' here to the stock was a bad idea I'm just realising. I'm tired and I can't concentrate because for the past couple of weeks I've been drivin' around and sleepin' in the car. I'm hittin' that pothole by the sign for The Meat Boutique and I'm twistin' and freewheelin' round and round, where I go no fucker knows.

'Ooh ooh ooh, another one bites the dust.'

And it's me they're talkin' about as I come to a stop after what seems like three and a half years of spinnin'. Mickey McCourt is headin' towards me with a fire extinguisher and before I have a chance to tell him to stick it up his arse I'm blasted in the face with ten tonnes of foam. It's like being spunked by an elephant. I'm easin' my way out of the sun roof because the doors jammed, and then I spot them. The three of them. McManus, Doot and Shawshank. Standin' there in the background giving it the silent salute. Lookin' at me with wee quizzical grins. I'm pickin' out Shawshank and there's this moment between us. There's this fraction of a minute where no one else is in the picture. There's a twitch in his grin as he tries to bat back the stare that I'm loadin' at him. He stops smilin', tries to look like a hard cunt and then turns away into his pint. Cool as fuckin' polar bears except for the wee pink twinge in the apples of both his cheeks.

Fuck this, I'm thinking as I'm makin' my way to the other end of the bar. Who's standin' holdin' up the bar with his left knee, only her da. Christ, this is all I need.

'Here, son, let me buy you a drink. That was bad luck out there.'

I'm trapped now, back to the bar and his face swayin' away in front of mine.

'Pint of Budweiser.'

He has that bloated, shiny, stretched face of your serious alcho, like the face on a broken doll, as if, if you poked it too hard it would crack, like cheap burnt cheese on a piece of toast.

'How's your Sandra? Sandra, that's your eldest's name, isn't it?' God, I'm a cunt.

'Ah, for fuck's sake. You probably see more of her than I do. She's never out of that garage.'

'I must pop in sometime for an oil change. She's great at the oul' oil changes.' Cunt cunt cunt.

A wee confused cloud flickers over his face, and then he remembers he's just a pisshead and starts laughing at fuck-all. Just then I want to smash his face off the bar. Watch that dead-doll face split wide open and dribble red all over the mahogany veneer.

But I'm feeling a bit Chris Tarrant, so I don't actually want to do that. I give him another lifeline and just turn my back on him, pint and all.

Sinead The noise of the car woke me up. I'd gotten that used to not hearing it for the past while I got a shock. There was the *Close Encounters* light show, then the handbrake, but then nothing. For a good long hour there's nothing, then I hear him make his way into the house. He drops his keys, and then again nothin'. For a good hour again there's nothin'. At the end of this good long hour I've had enough. I have to go downstairs and see what he's up to but when I get there he's just sittin' at the kitchen table with his head in his hands. There's a

stink of petrol off him and he's warbling on about how
he's goin' to be a better man and how he loves us all
really and how there are going to be changes round here
and how he really does appreciate me. I ask him where
he's been for the past two weeks and he says he's been in
Hell for the past fortnight. He's been sleepin' in the car
and drivin' round and just thinkin'. I ask him, 'What's
"Hell"? Is it some brothel out in Carrickmacross?', then
close the kitchen door and go back to bed. The bed with
the invisible barbed-wire down the middle, the same bed
I sit on the edge of and dig my nails into the palms of my
hands. I'm drawin' blood because this is how it's been for
the past two weeks. He's been away from the house
sleepin' in his car. He looks at me with panic eyes and
of course I'm askin', does he know? Is this his way of
tormentin' me with some passive-aggressive man tease-
thing he's picked up off the TV? Why doesn't he just
come out with it? What's all the constipated eyeballs
and wringing' his hands? I'm goin' off my lid here. The
bastard. I've Joseph Mengele crossed with Mr Spock
interrogatin' away through Vulcan mind-melds down in
the sitting room and if our oven was gas, in my head
would go.

Hammy So I'm standing in front of Shawshank's truck
with a jerrycan full of kerosene. I'm up round Camlough
Lake and there's night birds and reeds on the water and
fuckin' crawlin' animals of all sorts to my left and to my
right. All disturbed from their wee nocturnal habits by
four tonnes of flatbed and me. David Attenborough'd
have a fit and so will Shawshank for that matter. I stayed
for just the one in the bar after all. Just lookin' at her da
and lookin' at the lads and lookin' at my hands and
thinkin', 'Some people just get a raw fuckin' deal in life.'
And amn't I the fuckin' master-dealer? Shufflin' away like
a bastard and flickin' them raw-deal cards in the
Pumpgirl's face? Shawshank's grinnin' away over there

and the lads are laughin' at the tops of their voices, but it's just that wee bit too loud, too self-conscious, you know? So down the pint goes on the mahogany veneer and swayin' Billy here waves a bye-bye as I make my way through the crowd. As I get to the door, McManus turns towards me and heads that wee bit too close to danger territory all right, and says, 'You headin' so soon?' And I looks him in the eye and blows him a kiss and says, 'Aye, I am. I'm away to have a wee fuckin' word with your wife.' Shawshank's rictus grin must be makin' his teeth ache to fuck at this stage, but they let me walk by out into the moonlight and the car park where things are parked. Cars and the like. Flatbeds and such things.

There's not one sinner about except maybe the souls of a few Brit soldiers as I empty the contents of the jerry the length and breadth of the truck. Up I gets into the cab and off with the handbrake and as she rolls her way down the hill, her big back-end creakin' with the effort, one wee flick of my Zippo is all it takes. With a cross between a pop and a bang she lights up the black, rolls into the lake and settles on the water for a minute like some Pawnee Indian burial. I sit there watching, my chin on my knees as her big arse dips under the water, first one side then the other, with a fizz and a snuff and a huge buckled groan at her death.

Pumpgirl Bumped into him yesterday in the town. Was walkin' past McLogan's and there he was, large as life with the wife and the two kids. Never seen him with her before. He's never with her. 'Why's he with her?' I'm thinkin'. Mr Big-Fat-Family-Man. She didn't see me, but he did. Looked at me funny, probably on account of me lookin' different. I've a skirt and sandals on and I put the baseball hat in the bin. Hammy coughs and puts his arm round his wife, the way men do when they're afraid of being caught on lookin' at other women. He stopped short of giving her a kiss on the cheek though. Ran his fingers through the wee boy's hair. But his eyes are on me. I forget the wee boy's name. I don't think he's ever told me. They all turned up the corner into Buttercrane shopping centre and his wife stops to get something out of her bag. He turns round and looks at me again, but she doesn't notice and they move off. I follow them round Buttercrane, like this film I remember watchin'. There were zombies in this shopping centre in America. I'm the biggest zombie in the place. They stop outside the jewellers and I'm across the way. Hammy's looking straight at me in the reflection in the glass. My knees are shakin' as his wife makes her way into the shop. I'm wonderin' should I go up to talk to him, but his look says not. It says lots of things. It says to me anyway: 'I can't talk to you for whatever reason. I can't see you. Don't come near me, not now, not with her around. Not with the kids here. You know I love my kids.' That's what his eyes are saying in the reflection, bouncing off a load of Claddagh rings and official Man U jewellery. I'm trying to say 'It's okay but I miss you' with my eyes, and someone walks past, barging into me. 'Get out of the fucking way, blue legs.' And he's gone, into the shop, behind her, behind the kids.

Sinead It's like he's been cloned. It's him but it's not him. It's like havin' another shadow. One that moves of its own accord. Everywhere I turn he's there, lookin' back at me. Smilin' away. It's very unnervin'. Two weeks of him not coming near the house and now I can't get rid of him. Following me around like a lost wean. For the few hours a day he goes to work in the hatcheries it's like peace descends on the place again. Then there'll be that horn goin' and he'll appear at the door with yet another type of poundshop sweets for the kids. Our Diane had a visit last week and sat with her jaw on the floor. Asked me if I believed in aliens. I laughed but I can see her point. There was a film on last night. Jodie Foster and him with the gerbil up his arse. Gere. Richard. He was her husband and went off to fight in the American Civil War or somethin' and came back, only he was completely changed. A different person. Used to be a right bastard but now he's lovely. Buildin' fences and buying her bonnets. I wonder if he got them in the poundshop.

Hammy I was just standin' there lookin' at her reflection in the glass. I'm trying to avoid her but I can't, you see, because there's this burnin' on the back of my neck. Sinead's not noticin' anythin'. Our eldest, Kelly, turns around and spots her. 'There's that one from our estate,' she says. Kelly's wavin' an ice cream and the top falls off, landin' at her feet. Up comes this wail and I have to promise her I'll get a new one. Just right now I want to slap her, and maybe I'm a bit rough because Sinead pulls her away from me and looks at me like I'm demented. I'm pretendin' to look at a tray of sovereign rings you could float a family on, but I'm checkin' out behind me, starin' at her across the way. She's not wearin' what she's usually wearin' and it occurs to me that I've never seen her outside work. Fuck. She looks like she's gonna come over. She's about to move but someone barges into her with a trolley, laughin', sayin' somethin', hurtin' her, again. And she looks hurt, she does. And I want to smash her face in. And I want to smash his face in too, the bastard with the trolley, but most of all I want to put my own face through the glass in front of me, again and again back and forward, and lacerate my head to bits. I want to see all of me dripping down over cheap love-token jewellery shite. But I don't smash my head at all. I just stand there watchin' the ice cream melt. Watchin' the raspberry sauce getting' wider and wider until it's pink and it makes me feel sick. Sinead's away into the shop now, a puzzled look on her face. I'm smilin' away like an eejit and I look up and the Pumpgirl is talkin' to some wee woman. She's tryin' to look past her to me, but the woman blocks her view. So I'm gone into the shop leaving her behind and the ice cream plopped on the ground.

Pumpgirl And that's it, he's gone with his wife and kids into the shop. I'm standing there in the middle of Buttercrane, and there's all sorts of thoughts goin' zippin' around my head. She must have found out or something. It's her, isn't it? She's raised the shit and he can't leave. Because of the kids. He loves them to bits. If it wasn't for them he'd have left her. That's why he hasn't been round. Because he wouldn't just not come round. He's my friend. I'm glad he's my friend. There's no one in the world like Hammy. Me and Hammy talk for hours. We do. And he would tell me not to mind the cunt with the trolley, but he can't because of his kids, and I'm dizzy in the shopping centre now. People are going past me and looking at me weird. I'm number-one fucking-zombie-queen now all right, just wandering about banging into people. Some wee woman asks me if I'm okay, and there's this music pumping out of HMV Records and it's AC/DC, 'Back in Black'. Everyone's starin' at me, but maybe they're not, and there's wee lads laughin' away but maybe they're not either, and I can't tell if they're all cunts or not. I tell the wee woman to fuck off out of it and head out the door and across the road weaving through the cars that are dootin' away, away over to the canal and breathe in and out the fresh air really fast because if I don't I'll throw up into the water below.

Sinead 'Are you awake? Are you awake?' This is what he comes out with last night. I'm lying there dead as Hector and he's whisperin' in my ear with this jabbin' finger. *Jab, jab, jab.* I think I've gotten away with it, let him think I go into a coma when I'm in the bed when he slips in between the covers. And there it is again. That *jab, jab, jab.* 'Are you awake, Sinead honey?' Honey! I make a *hrumph hrumph* sound before he leaves a bruise on my shoulder *jab, jab, jab, jab. Hrumph hrumph, jab*, but my eyes are goin' ninety with the panic. He snuggles into my back and there's this hairy arm wrapped round my waist and a hand on my breast and I'm about to have a stroke.

He's peckin' away at the back of my neck now. *Peck, peck.* 'Did you ever think, *peck slurp peck*, that it might be a good time *peck peck nibble,* to think about having another *slurp peck squeeze* BABY? *Slurp.*' And I'm rigid now, transfixed. The whole right-hand side of my face is soaked, so I mention something about having my monthlies so he stops, abrupt like, and I think he's gonna pull away to the other side but he doesn't. He lies there with his arm round my waist, pressing on my stomach. And I want to rip his arm off and toss it to the dog. I want to jump up and bounce up and down on the bed *bounce bounce* and shout, 'You can't have a baby, you stupid man. You can't, you know. Because of course *bounce bounce* you see, you stupid fucker, there's already one there.' He lies there with his arm round my waist, pressing on my stomach which presses on my bladder, giving me a massive urge to pee. I don't sleep a wink all night.

Hammy I was treadin' water in the deep end of this massive indoor pool. It was my first time out of the shallow end and I'd made my way round there bit by bit every now and again taking my hand off the side and feeling the nothing underneath, so then grabbing back quickly, but I'm feeling really brave and it's okay, you know? Nothing to it. So there I am at the side and I turn round and splash my feet in front of me and have a good look around. All the fellahs round me seem much bigger than me, so I turn away again, dip my head under the water and when I come up again there's plasters and bits of hair and scab tops in the drain bit just level with my nose. I turn round again to get away from this, and everyone seems to be far away up the other end, like it's the biggest pool in the world and there's nothin' but the loud noise of feet splashin' all round me. Then something catches the corner of my eye and there's a load of guys hanging on to this giant rope, and I think I can see McManus among them. These guys are pulling on this rope and there's this sound and I begin to lose my grip on the drain and I'm being sucked down into this massive plughole. I'm caught up in all the hair and the scabby bits of skin and condoms and other fuckin' horrors as we head towards this huge gurgling hole. And everyone else gets out of the pool easy, but I'm trapped in the fuckin' grossest slipstream of a current in the world.

And then I wake up covered in sweat and the clock on Homer Simpson's arse on the alarm to my right says it's four o'clock in the morning and I realise that I've just come within an inch of wettin' the bed.

Pumpgirl The school is next to the where the barracks used to be. I went there myself and we'd get free days on account of bomb scares. On bomb-scare days the convent up the road evacuated all the nuns apart from the really old ones. I used to sit and think about old nuns in beds, lying there waiting for a bomb to go off, wonderin' if it was a hoax or the real thing. The smell of that oul' convent the last thing going through your head along with probably a massive piece of masonry.

It's the first day back at school and the weans are out for dinnertime. The girls are playing German jumps and every now and again some wee lad jumps in and twists round the elastics, snapping them and leaving welts on the legs of the two wee girls at either end, one of which is Hammy's, don't know her name. He never told me. She's got her wee red cardigan wrapped round her waist and her sleeves rolled up and she's tellin' this young fellah to fuck off. Round the corner stands her wee brother, a skinny wee boy with Hammy's walk. He's being made to pick up litter with another wee lad and he's well pissed off. The two of them have yellow marigold gloves on and the caretaker stands watching them, telling them how to be an expert in litter-picking-up.

Sinead The wee humpy woman from the shoe stall grabs a pair of Nike Air Max and clutches them to her chest protectively as I pass her. It's early on in the day. Not my usual five o'clock saunter. The weather's Irish warm and sticky. Tempers short. No time for loiterers. I'm a nuisance now, I think, just wanderin' round and not buying anything. That weird one who just gets in your way and smokes over the stock. But I pay them no mind. I'm here for one thing. There's a fruit shop at the front entrance and Mr Glamour Shawshank himself is unloadin' a dose of plums from a clapped-out Mini Metro.

'Traded in the oul' flatbed, then?' says I, to make polite conversation.

He turns as if he's been shot. Point blank through the back of the neck. Bit of an over-reaction, I'm thinkin', which is kinda reinforced when I see the look on his face.

'Are you doin' your bit for the environment then? Cuttin' down on the oul' emissions?'

He's lookin' at me like I'm an almighty punishment squad, and isn't he the IRA punishee about to find himself up a ditch somewhere lookin' at his nuts in a black plastic bag? He drops his plums, I kid you not, and stands there blinkin' away. This is not how I had expected this to go. I mean, it's hardly *Dr Zhivago*, you know? We stand there like two kids watching a piece of fruit on the ground roll down the trace of the gutter and settle itself behind a pickled-onion Monster Munch bag.

Hammy The kids are magic, you know? I swear, they're fantastic craic. No, seriously, I could turn off the TV and sit and watch the two of them for hours, breaking my shite laughin'. I never noticed before. Darren's a sketch. He's the image of me at that age and it's mad, you know? Watchin' a carbon copy of yourself even down to the wee walk and everything. Kelly now, she's as sharp as a splinter. She's not like the wife though. Not quiet. She's a talker and she has this mad imagination. The things that come out of that wee girl's head. Fantasies. Stories of ghosties and all. Maybe she takes after me, too. That can happen, can't it? She makes up all these wee plays with her dolls and she's as choosy. I got them stuff from Poundworld in the town. A Spiderman mask hood thing for himself and a wee doll for her. He was as happy, runnin' off pretendin' to have webs in his hands, thwack thwack. But she's goin', 'No way, Daddy. Its Bratz dolls or nothin'.' And she's all sincere, you know? All wee frown and lookin' at me with these clenched fists. And I'm lookin' at this wee frowny face and down-at-the-sides mouth, and there's him thwackin' his way round the garden and this feelin' starts to make its way up my legs, into my bones. I'm lookin' at the two of them, and I have to hang on to the wall because I'm shakin' like a mad thing and leanin' over, dry retchin'. Kelly asks me if I'm okay, Daddy, and I say I am, but I'm not. I'm not at all. There's a boilin' feelin' in my belly like I'm hungry but at the same time full up with greasy shit food. Darren's trying to climb the side of the house now, so I tell him to get down to fuck. Kelly's lookin' like she's gonna cry and she's pulled the head off the Poundworld Suzie from China so I promise her I'll get the Bratz doll and as I'm managing to get myself to the car I'm sayin', 'Now come on to fuck, yous are late for school.'

Pumpgirl There's no way I'd have kids, you know? You spend all your time bringin' them up and teachin' them right from wrong and how to be safe and then they go off with the first person they see. They should ban kids and ban ice cream too. They'll do anything for an ice cream, won't they? Even in the middle of winter. Ice-cream van comes into any estate, there's sixty of them runnin' up the road after it. Ice-cream vans is mad. I mean, is there a factory somewhere that makes ice-cream-van musical instruments? Could you buy one for the house or something? I'm thinkin' all these mad things as we're walkin' the viaduct way home. Me and Hammy's two kids, eatin' ice cream. It's Pooh Bear from a posh shop and it's got big lumps of honeycomb goin' through it. I sat by the school all day watchin' them, listening to them doing their five times tables and tellin' God how much they loved him. Then at half past two they're let out, and I'm watchin' them just standin' at the gate. No one seems to be pickin' them up. Everyone else, all the school mams and the odd da pickin' up the other kids, but they just standin' there. The boy has a Spiderman mask on and he's clingin' to the railin's. The wee girl looks lost and she looks straight at me. They know me from the estate and it's a sign, you know? That there's no one there to meet them, so over I walks.

Sinead 'There's two Francis Bacons,' I blurt out, and there's silent gunshot number two, straight through the hook of his eyebrow, which is raised, quizzical like, terrified. 'Whaaa . . . t's that?' he says. 'There's two Francis Bacons,' I says, and one of his eyebrows ricochets off the other.

'I googled him and there's two of them, an artist and a poet, the artist was Irish, you know. And just as I'm about to weep with embarrassment at the irony of the most pregnant pause in the country, doesn't the shopkeeper appear, the wee woman from behind the shoe stall, Christ maybe she's his ma, pops her head up as if to say, 'Yous needin' an interpreter there at all and mind you keep your dirty hands off my Reeboks.'

I turn and walk away, leaving them starin' after me. Not quite the reaction I was expectin', but there's men for you. And anyway I was only coming here for a last look. A last look at the father of my child.

Pumpgirl Through the viaduct walk, past the water plant with about eighteen magpies rattlin' away. I start singin' 'One for sorrow, two for joy,' and the wee girl asks me what I'm singin'. She's called Kelly. I tells her it's a song about countin' and she smiles. There's ice cream all over her face, so out comes the sleeve. The wee boy Darren has his Spiderman hood halfways up his face and eatin' his ice cream. 'Are you a boy or a girl?' says he, but I only smile back because he's just a kid. 'C'mon,' says I. 'Come on and I'll show yous the upside-down house. The one at the back of the viaduct.' 'The what?' says them both at the one time, which was funny. 'The upside-down house,' says I. 'Fuck off,' says he. 'There's no such thing as an upside-down house. An upside-down house would fall over or something. Ha ha. You're fuckin' mental.' 'Stop swearin',' says she, 'or I'll tell Ma on ye.' Her mentionin' the cunt-wife makes me want to slap her hard, but I don't because then she'd run away and squeal. Instead I takes them both by the soft baby arm and leads them under the viaduct and over the main road. I'm sayin', 'There's an upside-down house just over here and there's cows livin' in the top half, I swear I'm tellin' the truth.' And there is. I've been there before and I'm thinkin', 'With yer da.'

Sinead But he follows me outside. There's a shop round the back of the market with a sign saying 'We Buy – stroke – Sell Anything' and I'm wondering do they do a line in babies when there's this polite cough and a hand on my shoulder. Well, it would be a polite cough, only it's a bit too forced and he nearly brings up a lung in my ear as I flinch my way towards him. It's funny how people can smile with their mouth and not with their eyes, because that's what he's doing, and there's a grip on my arm as his tongue presses against what are teeth like a basket of chips in his mouth.

'I'm sorry,' says he. 'You just took me by surprise there.' The grip lessens a bit and becomes a rub on the arm, but not a sexy rub, oh no. More like you'd rub a kid with a sore knee. The eyes is dartin' about and I'm wonderin' if the wife is around. But I'm a cocky bitch and I am having his kid so I says, 'I think you and me should have a little chat.'

Now I go from havin' what I think is the upper hand here to nearly havin' the hand wrenched off me. He leads me by the elbow back round to the Mini Metro and bundles me inside. 'How's about a fuckin' spin then?' says he, so I says, 'Seein' as you put it so poetically how could a girl resist?' But as sexy banter goes I'm thinkin' this has got to be up there with the worst. He starts up the engine and as he drives off, eyes dartin' dart-dart, he misses the wee Romanian woman by three inches. And that's us cursed to fuck in Romanian for the rest of our lives. I try to settle myself into the car as he reverses out, trying not to look at his hands on the wheel. His hands in the perfect twenty-to-two position that I know from Hammy driving, trying to look ever so calm when inside he's as nervous as fuck.

Hammy I mean, I can just have a word with her, can't I? Nothin' threatenin', just talk to her. Sort things out, or should I leave her the fuck alone? I don't know what to do. My hands are slippery on the steerin' wheel as I turn the corner into the kids' school. 'Right, bye-bye, and no fuckin' messin' around,' I says, and big nods from the two of them. I drive around for a couple of hours still thinkin' about maybe headin' up to the garage just to see if she's there but I can't face them grey green slanty eyes. I say fuck it and head up there anyway. I slow-burn past the pumps, but I can't see her, only the other one. The one with the candyfloss perm that shouts back your order from behind the counter. I haven't got the balls to go in. Fuck it, I'll cruise about a bit more, get the child's doll

and then go to work. There's all sorts of scenarios
poppin' into my head. Shawshank, Doot, McManus.
Fuck, he's the wife's brother-in-law, but I'm being stupid.
They'll say fuck-all and her, no I don't think she'll say
anything, so I should be breathin' easy, but I'm not.
Because she's not the real problem, is she? Is she? I'm not
breathin' easy at all. I'm barely breathin' at all as I turn
into the hatcheries. I realise I've forgotten all about the
child's doll. I've gone straight to work instead. I'm early, so
I just sit in the car with the window up. Sweat's pumpin'
off me now. I look like someone from one of them old
war films in the jungle with big patches of sweat under
each arm waitin' for the Japs to make me finish buildin' a
fuckin' bridge or something. It's mad hot for September
I'm thinkin', as I step out of the car and it just makes the
smell of chickenshit rise to smack me in the nostrils.

Sinead Now here's the thing about the road we're on for
the spin. It's a windey fucker, you know? Gyrates and
twists like your Uncle Tommy doin' the Hucklebuck. Not
the best if you're in the throes of morning sickness.
Especially if you've Eddie Irvine here sitting beside you
at the wheel.

'Could you not slow the fuck down or what?' says I,
and he does. So sudden I'll be putting in a claim for
whiplash. He crawls along the road and as I can't tell him
to speed the fuck up again I settle into the seat catching
him looking at me and then looking at the road and then
looking at me. We stop behind a car which is turning into
an old clapped-out petrol station and as I'm wondering
if there's a poem about awkward silences, who do I spot
coming towards us, on the other side of the road but my
husband. And he's going slow. Real slow. He hasn't seen
us because he's cruisin' past and starin' into the garage.
Shawshank hasn't seen Hammy because for some reason
he's staring into the garage too. Starin' intently over my
shoulder as we're stopped behind this car. I'm watchin'

Hammy's car up ahead, Hammy's car comin' for us at half a mile an hour and I'm wondering if there's a special offer on in the garage as the car in front finally makes its turn. Shawshank's looking over my head and then at me and I'm thinking at this rate the two cars could pass and have the divorce papers signed on the bonnet and before I know what I'm doing, before I can stop myself, my hand lashes out and jerks the steering wheel forcing the car and a very put-out Shawshank off the road and safely incognito-like into the petrol station forecourt.

Pumpgirl And I wasn't lettin' on. There is an upside-down house round the back of the viaduct and across the road. I don't know what it used to be, but now it's a house that's sort of grown into the countryside beside it so much that you can walk straight into the upstairs from outside. It's like this hill has grown up round it and there's cows wandering in and out through these old windows. There's a big hole in the middle where the top floor has given way and the only way down is down an old iron ladder someone's put up because the floor's totally rotted away and covered in ivy. 'Well, it's not upside-down,' says Mr Picky Darren. 'But it's good anyway. Them cows is mental.' 'Who bought you your Spiderman mask?' asks me, because I can't stand it any more. I'm dying to talk about Hammy so then it starts. Me askin' loads of innocent wee questions like all, 'And what does yer daddy think of that?' and 'Where was yer mammy then?' And they're answerin' all these questions while runnin' back and forward tryin' to scare the cows. The sunlight streams through the windows and the cows are runnin' everywhere as I'm learning all about the Hammy and the cunt-wife's new relationship. How Daddy's always around now and buying them presents like sweets and toys like Spiderman hoods and Bratz dolls. How one day last week he was askin' them both how they would feel about maybe havin' a new little

baby brother or sister. How would they feel about that?
How would they feel? They. Feel.

Sinead We sit there for ages just watching people going
in and out of the shop. Buyin' petrol, milk, doin' the
lottery, whatever. Watching hope on people's faces as
they fill in numbers of birthdays and houses and waist
measurements and numbers of significance, ticking boxes
for no publicity with as much care as you'd spend on a
will. Finally, achingly, just sitting there waiting for
something to say, out comes me.

'Are you not gonna get some petrol, then? Or did you
just come in here for the craic?'

There's a pause, and then he shifts, looking right into
my face and it's hot in the car, hot for September and the
heat makes me squirm and stick to my seat.

Hammy I was cleaning out the chicken coops. Chicken
coops is too good a name for what these are. Four to a
cage, beaks pecked off eating their own shite. No eggs
allowed in our house, that's for sure. I'm hosing down
the coops like I have to every six weeks and there's shite
everywhere. Shite and eggshells and bits of beak and
things from nightmares all heading towards this drain we
have in the middle of the yard. The water's full of stuck-
together feathers like some massive sodden living animal
moving towards this big black hole in the ground with a
pulse like, gross. And I'm blasting these hatches with this
hose and it's one of those big power ones, like a shotgun,
that would knock you off your feet, and all of a sudden
I turn it in another direction and blast the fuck out of
every fucking thing in that yard. There's eggs and shite all
over the place. One bird hits the wall with such a force
that its neck snaps and there's this strangled noise as
I have it pinned to the wall with a giant jet of water. I'm
screaming at the top of my lungs this fucking animal yell
and I'm smashing everything around me. Boxes upon
boxes of eggs splattered to fuck and panic-stricken birds

54

runnin' about trying to escape from me and my mighty weapon. And I start to laugh. I slide down the wall with the water gun in my hand just dribblin' now, and I'm laughin' so hard I think I'm gonna pass out, and I sit there for what seems like hours, every now and again laughing with the hilarity of it all.

Pumpgirl The cows have all gone now. All disturbed from their upside-down house and stumblin' down the side of the hill all pissed off because of the strangers in their big green living room. They're all huddled together in a clump now at the bottom and there's grey and black clouds creepin' over the sky. Kelly's on her back trying to make angels in the long grass but she's pissed off because it's not as good as snow. Darren's runnin' around lettin' on he's Spiderman. He's climbin' round the edge of the big hole in the floor, hangin' on to the old ivy roots and I go and stand behind him, quietly. There's this wee mole on the back of his neck with another tiny one. Looks like two wee planets or a planet and a moon. I'm close enough to him now, but he's no idea I'm there. The Spiderman hood is pulled down over his ears so the biggest thing he can hear is his own breathin' as he wraps his fingers through the really old bits of plant. Kelly's still behind me doin' angels in her own wee world so I'm there on my own. Wee shitface Darren here gets my full attention so for the minute she can just wait. I step further out with my foot. My foot makes a creak in the floorboards which makes him stop like a cat on a roof. His spidey sense is tinglin' all right as he lifts his head in the air and he can't get the hood off because he's still holding on to the ivy because if he doesn't he'll fall. And the hood's in his eyes now, slipped up, blinding him. We stand there for about a minute that's just like an hour with him near breaking his neck twisting round his head first to one side then to another trying to see who's behind him and the whole time I'm leaned over him with my face about two inches from his. Just watchin' his wee face twitchin' and jerkin' with the panic and the wee hands grapplin' and twistin' and tryin' to hold on to the roots. And it's deep, that drop behind him. Very deep. The height of three men.

Sinead 'I'll tell you what,' says he, still lookin' at me in the warm. 'How about we now have that wee chat?' He lets his tongue roll over the words 'wee chat', and I'm thinking severely to myself that a garage forecourt is not the place to introduce his son and heir, when this smell of petrol wafts through the window and fills the car. Sweet, sickly, like markers in school. The kind of smell your nose finds on its own, seeks out. If it had a colour it'd be violet or purple, that smell. Don't ask me why, it just would. I can feel my face go white as my hair follicles start to sweat on the top of my head with the rising nausea that's creeping its way up my belly. 'Something wrong?' he asks, lookin' severely as if indeed there is, and I fumble for the door handle to get out and away from the car and into a toilet, away from the purple puke pregnancy stink that I know from chubby felt-tips, five to a pack. 'I don't feel very well,' I says as I gets the door open. But he grabs the door and snaps it shut, leaning across me with an elbow in my breast. There's crunchin' and splatterin' of gravel and he careers out of the forecourt with a 'Think you're fuckin' smart, don't you?' And I'm too busy trying to keep the bile from rising into my mouth to wonder what the fuck's going on.

Pumpgirl The first plop is on the back of my neck. Like a smack or an egg on the side of your head at Halloween, splat wet, nearly lose my balance because I'm stooped down so low just over Darren's face. I have to steady myself and then another one lands with another splat right on the end of one of his nostrils and because his face is turned up he breathes it in, making him choke. He starts to cough and splutter and wobble like fuck on the edge of the beam and there's this noise beside me and

Kelly's standin' there screechin' about how she's scared and I grab her and him, and hold them tight by the arm. He takes off the hood and stares up at me and there's the three of us on the edge of that hole, that hole the height of three men. All stopped. We all stop. None of us moves. Hammy's kids. The cunt-wife's kids. Hammy's kids and me.

Hammy A 1970s Toyota Celica has no catalytic converter, so the exhaust fumes should work real fast. It's a short walk to my car from the wall where I'm sitting. I pick up a piece of tubing that's lying flung on the ground. I walk round the back of the car and down I go, attaching the pipe to the exhaust. It's one of them corrugated pipes, moves real easy, like a concertina I'm thinking, as I pass it through the passenger window. I open the driver door, get in and settle myself in the seat. flick on the engine and stick a CD in the player. Glen Campbell fills the car as the first of the fumes start to make their way up their squeezy tube journey and into my lungs. Glen Campbell's career was very hampered on account of him being labelled the housewives' choice. If we look at the range of his music when he was with Capitol, we can actually see a man of enormous varied musical talent. Far beyond the constraints of the title he was lumbered with.

(*Sings.*) 'By the time I get to Phoenix, she'll be rising.'

On account of the aforementioned lack of catalytic converter, by the time we get to fuckin' Albuquerque my head is startin' to spin. I lean back into the seat as the first of a few threatening rain clouds start to block out the sun above, and as I drift in and out of consciousness I spot these funny wee scratches on the roof above me. Funny wee scratches on the lining of the car. I'm puzzled by the scratches as my eyes are closing in my head and my mind thinks back through my life trying to figure out where they came from and I see my wife, my kids, the lads, the wife's sister, my ma and da and me as a kid kickin' a ball, but no clue to the scratches and by the time we make Oklahoma . . .

Sinead He has me on the ground now. Out of the car and on the ground and leaning over me, face against mine. Close, I can smell cigarettes and onions and tin. Out of the car, pulled up in a lay-by, flung on the ground and the belt off and wrapped around his fist. I should be glad, I suppose, to be away from the smell of the petrol, but I have to say no, no, I'm not. He's yellin' at me over and over to tell him what I know and I'm thinking through tears and snot and piss down my legs that as over-reactions go this one is fucking huge. He calls me a clever bitch and Hammy a smart cunt and smashes the buckle off the door of the car so in order to stop that next time being my head, out comes the truth. The facts. The baby, fuck you, you psycho, that's all I know, that's all I wanted to tell you, but I guess you've kind of spoiled it now. He stops what he's doing, the belt falls to the ground. He leans up against the car and as the metal Indian head at his feet flashes gently in the sunlight, the first of a series of low chuckles starts to form in the back of his throat.

Pumpgirl It's wee soft baby arms I'm holdin' in my hands. Soft tiny arms with bones moving inside two wee scraps of things that have done no harm to me. I haul them back from the edge of the hole and yell at them that it's fucking dangerous there and how could they be so fucking stupid. Darren looks at me, but whatever thought he's havin' in his head he's already forgotten as she's bringin' up this almighty wail of 'I wanna go home'. So I say 'Okay' and that's what we do. Down the side of the hill under the viaduct and past the magpies. Past the library van, past the spot where their da used to take me and I'd look at the scratches above me and the crisps on the seat beside me. The crisps that they would have ate in the back of the car. And on we head home. The two soaking wet kids and me. Darren wears his hood like a hat on top of his head, which makes him look like one of the seven dwarfs. I'm pullin' my hoodie up over the back of me and Kelly, but it makes no odds. We're soaked to the skin. I turn up the driveway into the estate. It's really lashin' down now. I stop at the end of their road because that's as far as I can go. I say bye-bye, but they don't even hear me as they're off runnin' up the road. I turn and head home out past the swings and the monkey bars and onto the back entry that connects their street to mine. I lift the latch on the back door of our house and in I goes.

Sinead The taxi back seems to take about four hours. After he left me in the lay-by I had to walk for miles before one stopped. Walkin' along the road like a drunk woman with my tights in shreds and blood on my knees. It's about three o'clock and I'm hopin' I haven't been missed. I kept trying the Hammy on his mobile but I can't get no reply so I hope to God the wanker's remembered he has to pick up the kids. And I'm sad. I feel sad, and I feel frightened in my ripped clothes and I feel like a fool. He just got into the car and drove off and left me. Laughed at me, picked up his belt and screeched off in the car. What a gent. We pull up at our house, and as I step out of the cab the first of a few drops of rain start to hit the ground all around me. There's that smell of wet pavements in sunlight and my legs are shaking as I make my way into the safety of my home. I open the front door and in I go. There's no one about so I head into the bathroom and run the taps for a bath. I make my way into the kitchen and get out a pot from the cupboard above the cooker. The gas comes on with a whoosh and I throw the match in the sink where it makes a fizz-plop sound and then goes to black. Hammy and the kids'll be home soon and I start to make the tea.

Blackout.